Black Fathers
&
Bright Futures

By Aaron Fields

Copyright © 2025 Aaron Fields. All rights reserved.

Published by The Write Perspective, LLC

All rights reserved. No part of this book shall be reproduced or transmitted in any form or by any means, electronic, mechanical, magnetic, photographic including photocopying, recording or by any information storage and retrieval system, without prior written permission of the publisher. No copyright liability is assumed with respect to the use of the information contained in this book. Even though every precaution has been taken in preparation for this book, the publisher/author assumes no responsibility for errors or omissions. Neither is any liability assumed for any damage that results from the use of the information in this book.

ISBN: 978-1-953-962-69-0

🧠 **Food For Thought:**

When it comes to addressing one of the most pressing health disparities in our communities------infant & maternal mortality, it's time for black fathers to become beacons of hope and change. It's imperative that black fathers demonstrate love, unity, and advocacy in creating a brighter and healthier future for the community.

Once upon a time, in a vibrant and loving community, lived a group of strong and caring Black fathers.

These fathers noticed something very important: Black mothers and babies weren't always getting the care they needed.

The fathers knew they had to help. So, they came together to protect the health of Black women and their babies.

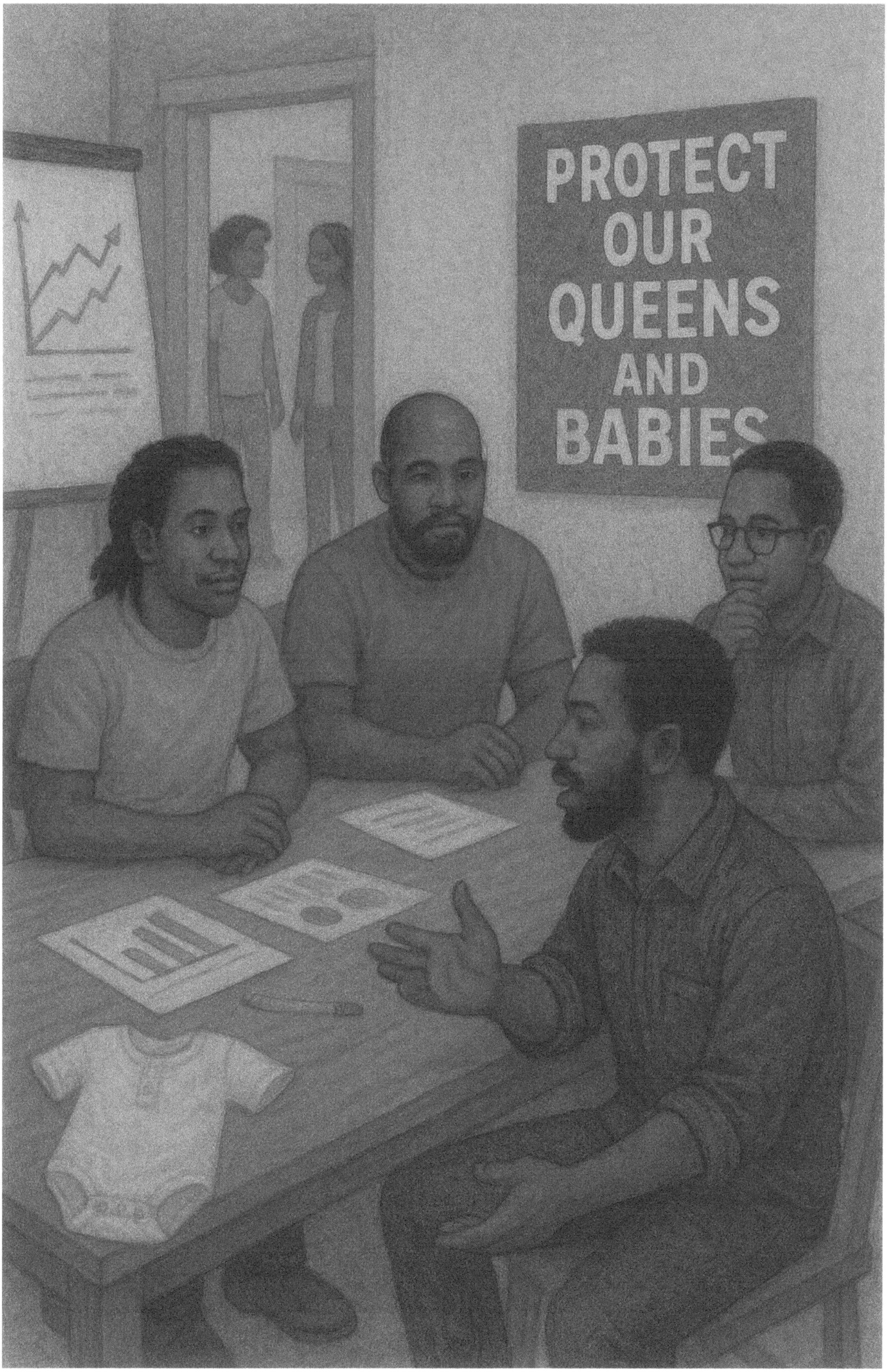
PROTECT
OUR
QUEENS
AND
BABIES

They spread the word about how important it is for moms to get check-ups during pregnancy.

They created support groups and safe spaces where Black women felt seen, heard, and cared for.

Some fathers went with moms to doctor visits, asking questions and learning how to keep moms and babies safe.

They reminded one another: "A healthy mama means a healthy baby."

They shared their own stories of fatherhood-----of love, fear, and the deep desire to protect.

The fathers hosted baby showers, health fairs, and fatherhood workshops----building strength through joy.

They were there for the hard days too, listening when mothers were scared, tired, or in pain.

They spoke to hospitals, leaders, and lawmakers to demand better care for Black women and babies.

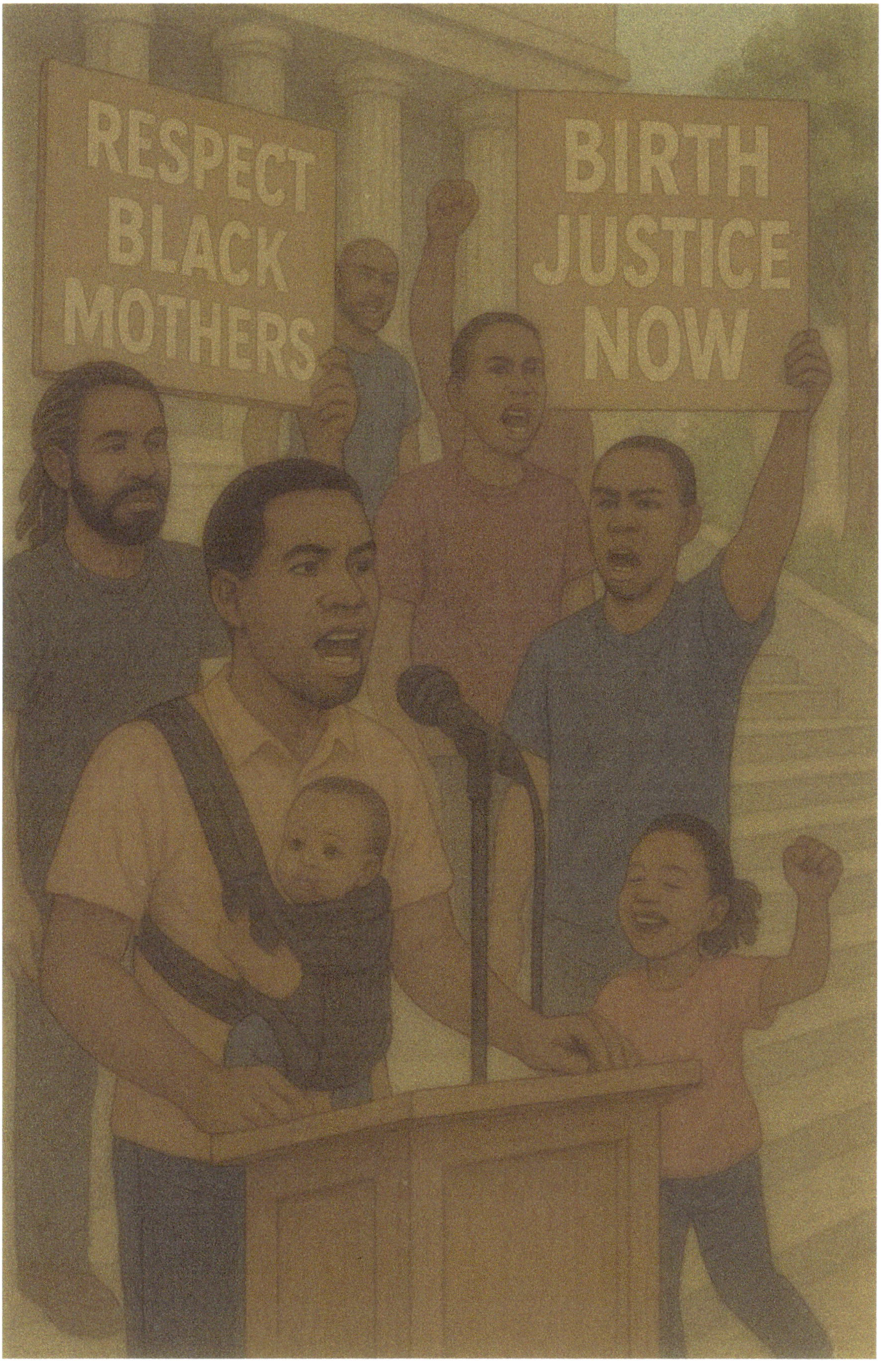
RESPECT BLACK MOTHERS
BIRTH JUSTICE NOW

Little by little, things started to change. Fewer babies were lost. More moms felt safe.

They didn't do it for fame. They did it because they loved their families and their community.

Their love created a legacy. One where Black fathers protect, nurture, and lead.

And so, the community grew stronger------with healthier moms, joyful babies, and fathers who stood proud and tall.

www.ingramcontent.com/pod-product-compliance
Lightning Source LLC
Chambersburg PA
CBHW041432040426
42450CB00021B/3471